BOLD KIDS

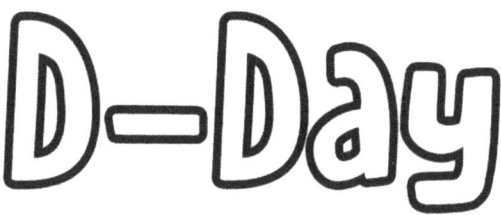

CHILDREN'S AMERICAN HISTORY BOOK

No part of this book may be reproduced or used in any way or form or by any means whether electronic or mechanical, this means that you cannot record or photocopy any material ideas or tips that are provided in this book. Copyright 2022

All images in this book have been reproduced with the knowledge and prior consent of the artists concerned, and no responsibility is accepted by producer, publisher, or printer for any infringement of copyright or otherwise, arising from the contents of this publication.

For children to understand the events of D-Day, it is helpful to look at a few facts about the battle. This historic event ended World War II and changed the lives of many soldiers, and it helped shape the public's perception of soldiers. These facts will help you explain the significance of D-Day to your kids.

Here are the interesting facts about D-Day for kids: First, DDay took place on the French Riviera. To reach the beaches, the Allies needed to cross the Atlantic. The Germans prepared their defenses using barbed wire, bunkers, and more than six million mines.

Second, learn about the D-Day invasion. This was the first of the D-Day landings. It took place during the night, and the Allied forces landed through Normandy. This was an incredible feat, and paved the way for a victory on the Western Front.

During the war, Allied troops fought for over two years in order to win the war. For these reasons, D-Day was an important day in history.

Third, learn more about the D-Day tank. This unique tank had a propeller that allowed it to swim. It was designed to move over land and into dense enemy defenses. Fourth, know about the Allied troops.

In total, over 24,000 US, British, and Canadian airborne forces landed in France on 6 June 1944. One-third of these troops landed safely, despite the fact that only one-in-six landed in the right place.

Lastly, know that the D-Day invasion began at night. The day-long invasion took place while the sun was still in the sky, making the fighting difficult and harrowing.

During the war, over 425,000 German and Allied troops died. The long-awaited movie 'The Longest Day' is based on Cornelius Ryan's 1959 book and tells the story of D-Day.

Invading Germany was not an easy task. In June 1944, the Allied forces captured the entire country. This war marked the end of World War II and the liberation of German-occupied Western Europe. The D-Day landings broke the Atlantic wall and allowed the Allies to liberate the continent.

By August 1944, Paris was free and the Allies gradually pushed eastward to Berlin. These events marked a turning point in the war.

D-Day took place in the morning on the French Riviera. Its first landing took place in darkness, but Allied planes launched 1467 sorties over the channel, and 126 aircraft were lost.

Almost one in six Allied paratroopers landed safely. These figures prove that the invasion of D-Day is a success for the Allies. But how did it happen? Here are some interesting facts about D-Day for kids.

During WWII, the Allied forces invaded the German-occupied coast of France. The battle was one of the deadliest battles of the war in Europe. The Allied forces landed on the Germanoccupied coast of Normandy and won the war.

By the time the Allies had conquered Germany, the Allied forces had conquered the entire country. This battle was an undisputed victory for the Allies.

The invasion began in the dark on D-Day. The Allied forces landed on the beach in the early morning of June 6th. The Allied forces had to overcome a vast number of obstacles in the area.

The battle was a major success for the Allies, and the Allied soldiers were able to successfully defeat the Germans. The first landing in Normandy was the largest seaborne invasion in history.

D-Day is a crucial date in the history of the war. The invasion took place in the dark on D-Day. In total, 13,000 men were killed during the battle. The Allied forces were able to capture most of the territory during the invasion, but the Germans were able to keep the majority.

The D-Day in France was the most successful military operation of World War II. It was the largest and most dangerous day of the conflict.

While the war was a big event, many Americans are unaware of how the invasion affected their lives. The Allies used the invasion as a springboard for their victory. In addition to this, they had to evacuate seven million tons of supplies to the UK.

The Americans were also able to send more than one million tonnes of supplies to the UK. The French Resistance was a major part of the invasion, and their actions were aimed at crippling the German forces.

Milton Keynes UK
Ingram Content Group UK Ltd.
UKHW050340100923
428316UK00007B/95